Table of Contents

Suggested Menus

Winter Holiday Tea

Steeped Tea
Cocoa Coffee
Tea Scones
Mim's Banana Bread
Marinated Mushrooms
Different Cheese Ball
Shortbread Cookies
Butterscotch Brownies

Formal Tea

Golden Tea Punch
Parmesan Cheese Rounds
Cucumber and Shrimp Sandwiches
Popovers
Lemon-Lime Curd
Gam's Graham Cracker Cake
Raspberry Squares with Raspberry Sauce

This book is dedicated to our mothers:

Barbara King
Muriel Schenkelberger
Carol Wagner

Our lives are fuller because of you and all
you've taught us. Simply put, your the cream
of the crop.

About The Authors

Between Friends is a collaboration of three very talented
women who are lifelong friends.
Pam McKee paints with watercolors and also hand letters the
calligraphy pieces found throughout each book.
Lin Webber is responsible for many of the finely detailed
watercolor vignettes spread among the text.
Ann Krum is a writer and cookbook collector.
All three live outside Philadelphia.

Afternoon Teas

Recipes - History - Menus

- by -
Pam McKee
Lin Webber
Ann Krum

A *Between Friends*® COOKBOOK

Fox Chapel Publishing • Box 7948 • Lancaster, PA 17604

All artwork © 1995 by Lin Webber and Pam McKee, used under license.
Text by Ann Krum
Editing: Beverly J. DeWitt
Typesetting and Copy Design: Dennis Shirk

ISBN# 1-56523-040-X

A Between Friends® Cookbook.
Fox Chapel Publishing Company, Inc.
Box 7948
Lancaster, PA 17604-7948
USA

Manufactured in Hong Kong

Suggested Menus

Informal Tea

Spiced Tomato Punch
Banana-Orange Muffin Cake
Boston Sandwiches
Pam's Apple Dip with Fruit
Quick Lemon Crisps

Summer Tea

Whitney's Almond Tea
Zucchini Bread
Fruit Platter with Yogurt Fruit Dip
Curry Cashew Sandwiches
Benne Seed Wafers
Fudge

You can taste and feel but not describe the exquisite state of response produced by tea—that precious drink which drives away the five causes of sorrow.

Emperor Chien Lung,
Manchu Dynasty

About Tea

A Brief History

Tea has been around so long that its precise origin as a beverage is not certain. According to Chinese legend, the Emperor Shen-Nung discovered tea when, in about 2500 BC, a few leaves from a nearby tea plant blew into the pot in which he was boiling his drinking water. The emperor enjoyed the flavor these leaves gave to the water, and tea as a beverage was born. However, a Chinese scholar named La Yu, who wrote the first history of tea in about 800 AD, claimed that tea was not common as a beverage until about the 6th century.

What is certain, however, is that Portuguese and Dutch traders were bringing back tea from China by the early to mid-1600s. The Russians, too, were importing Chinese tea in overland caravans. Although the English were to make tea famous, the first tea did not reach England until 1645, imported at exhorbitant prices from Holland. King Charles II helped make tea fashionable among the aristocracy in the 1660s, when he married a Portuguese princess whose dowry included this precious commodity. By the 1670s the famous East India Company was importing Chinese tea directly to England.

Tea began to usurp coffee's position as the beverage of choice among the English upper classes between about 1740 and 1800. Green tea was drunk, without milk, at breakfast and after dinner, often from expensive Chinese porcelain. English potteries soon started producing tea services, with such famous names as Wedgwood and Spode participating. And in the 1750s establishments called tea gardens—which served bread and butter with their tea—became popular gathering places for fashionable gentlemen. The price of tea remained high, however, due in no small part to the heavy taxes placed on it by the government. This levy made tea one of the most smuggled commodities of the time.

By 1840, the English had found a new source of tea: India. They began cultivating tea in the Assam area of northern India, first from Chinese seeds and later by domesticating wild Indian tea plants. This helped lower the price of tea and broaden its popularity.

By the 1850s, tea and light food were being enjoyed as a late-afternoon refreshment. In 1864 the first London tea shop opened for the service of afternoon tea, and afternoon teas were commonplace social occasions in polite society by the 1880s. By the 1890s, tea was the most popular drink in England. Today most Britons drink an average of four cups of tea a day, and the United Kingdom is the world's largest tea importer.

It is thought that tea first came to the colonies on Dutch ships that brought settlers to New Amsterdam. From there, its popularity spread throughout the colonies. But as it did in England, the government taxed tea heavily. The colonists' response was the 1773 Boston Tea Party, which set America on its course to becoming a nation of coffee drinkers.

Despite its preoccupation with coffee, however, America has made its own contributions to the world of tea. Iced tea was invented in steamy St. Louis at the 1904 World's Fair by a merchant who was distressed that people weren't buying his hot tea. He poured the tea over ice, and now people enjoy iced tea the year around.

The tea bag was also an American invention. A New York importer sent his tea about in silk bags. The idea caught on, and today tea bags are more common than loose tea in this country.

In the United States today, tea—and the customs and rituals associated with its drinking—are enjoying renewed popularity.

Tea Terminology

Tea plants—evergreen tropical bushes grown for their leaves—are cultivated for five years before the first harvest. At maturity, the leaves from the tips of the branches are picked every few weeks over a six-month period. The first picking of the season is considered the best. High altitudes produce better quality plants than lower locations.

After picking, tea leaves are allowed to wither (to dry slightly) in warm, dry air. They are then rolled to release moisture. The treatment the leaves receive from that point differs for the three types of tea: black, green, and oolong.

Types. To make black tea, the commonest type, the withered and rolled tea leaves are allowed to ferment fully before they are fired (dried) in ovens.

Green tea is made by steaming the withered and rolled leaves—without letting them ferment—before firing them. These leaves produce a green-colored, rather bitter infusion that has the least amount of caffeine of the three types. Green teas are especially popular in the Far East.

Oolong tea is partially fermented before being fired. This produces a rust- or copper-colored brew with an aroma like that of black tea but a flavor that is somewhat softer than that of green tea. Oolong tea also has less caffeine than black tea.

Grades. After firing, black tea leaves are graded by being passed through a series of increasingly smaller mesh screens. There are four grades (from largest to smallest leaf size/highest to lowest quality): leaf, broken leaf, fannings, and dust. There are also gradations within the leaf and broken leaf grades: flowery orange pekoe, orange pekoe, pekoe, and souchong. To most people's surprise, the term orange pekoe refers not to flavor or color but to a grade of tea. Fannings (and in some cases, dust) are used in tea bags so that the water can penetrate more quickly.

Categories. Teas are divided into two basic categories—China teas and India teas—reflecting the area in which the seed originated. Although India teas are today grown in locations as diverse as Africa, Indonesia, and Malaysia, as well as India and Sri Lanka (formerly Ceylon), the seed for these teas came originally from India. India teas are generally more robust than China teas.

China teas include Keemun (China and Taiwan), Lapsang souchong, Yunnan (western China), gunpowder, Formosa oolong (Taiwan), and jasmine. India teas include Assam, Darjeeling (a costly tea grown in the Himalayas), Nilgiri, and Ceylon.

All the India teas, as well as China's Keemun and Lapsang souchong, are black teas. Formosa oolong (a very expensive, low-caffeine tea considered by many to be among the world's finest) and the semi-fermented jasmine (which takes its name from the jasmine flowers it contains) are both oolong types. Gunpowder (the lowest in caffeine of all the teas) is a green tea.

Blends. To complicate tea terminology further, many of the names with which we are familiar describe blends rather than individual teas. These include Earl Grey (a blend of large-leafed China and India Darjeeling teas flavored with oil of bergamot), Russian Caravan (a blend of China teas), English Breakfast (a blend of India and Ceylon teas), and Irish Breakfast (a stronger blend of

India teas containing more Assam).

Spices and fruit peels are added to tea leaves to make spiced teas, and flavorful oils are sprayed on tea leaves to make flavored teas (like Earl Grey). Although called "teas," herbal teas are blends of herbs and flowers—not teas.

Tea Customs and Ceremonies

The English tradition of afternoon tea as a time for relaxation, refreshment, and socializing dates to the 1840s. It can be traced to Anna, the 7th Duchess of Bedford. One day, the duchess asked that a tray of tea and some bread and cakes be brought to her room about 4 PM, to tide her over until the customary 9 PM dinner hour. This practice spread among her friends. Over time, what began as one woman's late-afternoon pick-me-up developed into a social occasion.

Victorian ladies were judged by the quality of their afternoon teas. The menu generally included delicate sandwiches to take the edge off the appetite, breads or scones, jams, simple cakes, and sometimes elaborate sweets. Until Queen Victoria introduced the Russian custom of adding lemon to tea after a visit with one of her daughters there, the English generally took their tea with milk.

Although many believe that English high tea is a more formal version of afternoon (or low) tea, this is not the case. High tea simply means more substantial fare and a later hour. Generally served around 6 PM, high tea was marked by addition of one or more cooked dishes to the usual afternoon tea fare. Common among the Victorian working classes and in the country, high tea was a sit-down meal that replaced dinner. It is still common in country regions in the north of England and in

Scotland.

Cream tea originated in the western part of England (around Devon and Cornwall). Its name comes from the practice of serving the local clotted cream and jam with afternoon tea scones.

The nursery tea, or children's tea, was customary among upper class children in England. This was often a time when parents visited the nursery. The children were served bread, toast, or small sandwiches, along with cocoa or milk flavored with a little tea. Once or twice a week, they were also permitted a small slice of cake.

The custom of afternoon tea, whether in the drawing rooms of the upper classes or at one of the many English tea shops, remained strong in England until after World War II. The increasingly hectic pace of life—and some believe, the introduction of coffee bars in London's Soho in the early 1950s—are some reasons cited for its demise.

Although the recent interest in afternoon tea in this country is based on English customs, ceremony and ritual also surrounded the serving of tea in China and Japan. The Japanese, in particular, emphasized the aesthetics of tea-service and had formal rules governing the making and serving of tea. Garden teahouses were part of the Japanese tradition.

Afternoon Tea: American Style

Now that you know a bit about tea and its history, why not have an afternoon tea? Although we tend to think of "teas" as a woman's domain, there's certainly no reason to exclude men from these gatherings. You may want to make the fare a bit more robust, but not to the point of ribs or subs. After all, a tea is nothing if not gentile. It's white lace, flowers, and mannerly behavior.

It can be a step back in time, a reason for a woman to wear a hat or for a man to buy a seersucker suit. It can be for three best friends on a raw and rainy afternoon by the fire. It can be to introduce your children to something other than Nintendo, to entertain a visiting relative, or to show off a new grandchild. It can bring a neighborhood of divergent people together for a few hours, or it can announce an engagement. It can be for the groomsmen as well as for the bridesmaids, or it can simply be something different to do with the people in your bridge group or book club.

Teas can be as fancy as those at London's Ritz or as informal as you care to make them. This book aims at something in between. It offers suggested menus for four types of teas and provides recipes for edibles in four categories: teas and punches, breads and spreads, light servings, and sweets. You needn't be bound by any hard-and-fast rules about what to serve. Just think of a tea as an opportunity to enjoy good company, special friendships, and a bit of food—essentially, a chance to have a wonderful time!

Love and scandal are the best sweeteners of tea.

Henry Fielding

What is the matter with Mary Jane!
She's perfectly well and she hasn't a pain,
And it's lovely rice pudding for dinner Again!
What is the matter with Mary Jane!

When We Were Very Young
by A.A. Milne

Oh, my friends, be warned by me,
That breakfast, dinner, lunch, and tea
Are all the human frame requires . . .
Hilaire Belloc

Though we eat little flesh and drink no wine,
Yet let's be merry: We'll have tea and toast:
Custards for supper, and an endless host
Of syllabubs and jellies and mince pies,
And other such lady-like luxuries.
Percy Bysshe Shelley

We had a kettle: we let it leak:
Our not repairing it made it worse.
We haven't had any tea for a week . . .
The bottom is out of the Universe!
Rudyard Kipling

Polly put the kettle on,
We'll all have tea.
Nursery Rhyme

And youth is cruel, and has no remorse
and smiles at situations which it cannot see.
I smile, of course,
And go on drinking tea.
T.S. Eliot

Flowers make an afternoon tea special. Order something fancy
from the florist if you like, but remember that a few spring violets sprinkled on a white linen napkin or tied with a thin silk
bow can be just as charming.

Tiny vases each filled with two lilies of the valley and a bit of myrtle make delightful decorations.

A bowl of holly and greens makes a pretty centerpiece for a winter tea.

Mums and small sprigs of fall leaves make an autumn tea special.

If you must serve a sugar substitute, open the packets and pour them into a small china bowl. Provide a tiny spoon.

Don't trim all your sandwiches. Some people like the crust.

If you serve a special tea blend, wrap up a few servings and tie with a lace ribbon. Give a packet to each guest.

A tea is the perfect occasion to bring out your mother's collection of old teacups. They needn't match. Odd sets are much more interesting.

Few people today have a tea service. Try to borrow or beg one from a friend. If you fail, a china teapot will do just fine. As a matter of fact, James Beard says that tea should be made only in a china pot.

Dampen small clusters of grapes, roll in granulated sugar, and use them as an edible decoration.

When lemons are cheap, buy a lot of them, squeeze the juice into ice cube trays, and freeze. Wrap lemon cubes individually to use the rest of the year.

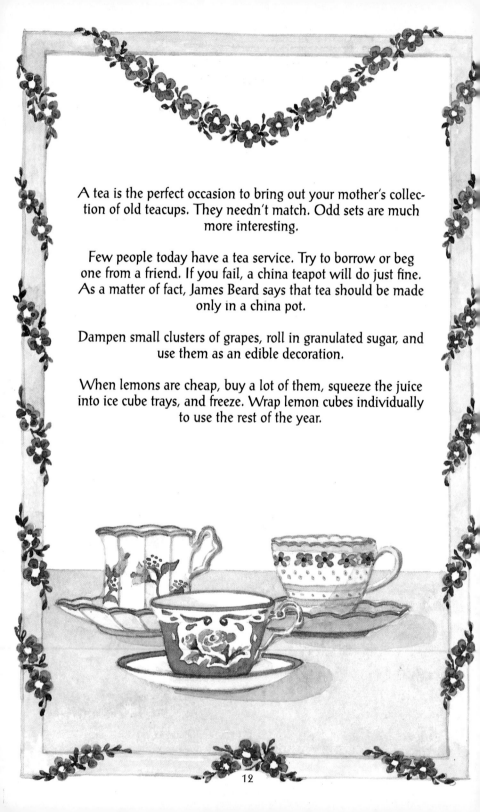

Teas
&
Beverages

GOLDEN TEA PUNCH

2 rounded teaspoons instant tea
2 cups water
1/2 cup sugar
3 cups orange juice
1 cup lemon juice
1 cup pineapple juice
1/4 cup grenadine
1 quart ginger ale

Stir tea into water until dissolved. Add sugar and stir until dissolved. Add juices and chill. To serve, place an ice mold in a punch bowl. Pour tea mixture into bowl; add grenadine and ginger ale. Serves 18.

SPICED TEA

18 ounces orange breakfast drink powder
1 cup sugar
1/2 cup instant tea
1 teaspoon cinnamon
1/2 teaspoon ground cloves

Add ingredients, a little bit at a time, to blender container and blend to a fine powder. Store in an airtight jar. Use 2 teaspoons mixture per serving for either hot or cold tea.

Dedhamware Pottery
Made in Dedham, Massachusetts
at turn of century - Originals are coveted
antiques & very expensive.

WHITNEY'S ALMOND TEA

5 regular tea bags (if you like strong tea, use more bags)
2 cups boiling water
1 cup sugar (1 1/2 cups if you have a sweet tooth)
1/3 cup lemon juice
1 teaspoon almond extract
1 teaspoon vanilla extract
2 quarts water

Place tea bags in a very large pitcher and pour the 2 cups of boiling water over them. Cover and steep 5 to 7 minutes. Remove tea bags. Add sugar, lemon juice, and almond and vanilla extracts; stir until sugar is dissolved. Add the 2 quarts of water.

RUSSIAN TEA

12 whole cloves
6 cups water
6 teaspoons loose tea
2 1/2 cups pineapple juice
Juice of 2 lemons
1 teaspoon grated lemon zest
Juice of 2 oranges
Sugar (to taste)

Add the cloves to the water, bring to a boil, and boil for 15 minutes. Remove from heat, add tea, cover, and steep 2 to 4 minutes. Strain. Add remaining ingredients. Serve hot.

STEEPED TEA

According to James Beard, tea must be made in a china pot, never in a teacup. Tea will not steep in a cup; the flavor and aroma escape.

First fill the teapot with boiling water to heat it. Empty the teapot and immediately add 1 teaspoon tea leaves per cup of tea. (Use a little more tea if you like your tea strong, but do not use less if you prefer your tea weak. Instead, add hot water to the tea after you have poured it into your cup.) Now pour boiling—not close to boiling or very hot, but boiling—water over the tea leaves. Put the top on the teapot immediately, before any steam escapes, and cover the pot with a tea cozy or a pretty dish towel. Allow the tea to steep for about 5 minutes.

SPICED TOMATO PUNCH

2/3 cup granulated sugar
1/2 teaspoon ground nutmeg
1/2 teaspoon cinnamon
Several whole cloves
1 quart tomato juice
1/2 cup lemon juice
2 cups hot water

Mix together sugar and spices; add to tomato juice in heavy saucepan. Bring to a simmer, stirring, to dissolve sugar. Add lemon juice and water; let simmer briefly to blend flavors. Chill before serving.

LEMONADE-MINT PUNCH

1/4 cup mint jelly
1 can (6 oz.) frozen lemonade
concentrate, thawed slightly
1 quart chilled ginger ale

In a large pitcher, mash jelly with a
fork. Add concentrate and mix well.
Add ginger ale and ice cubes. Mix
well. Serve in 4 tall glasses.

COCOA COFFEE

Combine 1 quart freshly brewed, chilled coffee with 1 quart prepared, chilled cocoa. Pour over ice in tall glasses. Serve with a dollop of whipped cream.

MINTED TEA

3 tablespoons fresh mint leaves
5 tablespoons loose tea leaves
3 thin strips lemon peal
1 tablespoon granulated sugar or honey

Bruise mint leaves well; place in non-metal teapot with remaining ingredients. Bring 1 quart water to a rolling boil. Immediately pour into teapot; let steep 5 to 7 minutes. Pour through a strainer to serve. Makes 4 cups.

FLOWER OR FLAVORED TEAS

To add a subtle aroma and flavor to teas, add fragrant flower petals—such as roses, gardenias, or violets—to tea leaves in a canister. Or place a vanilla bean among the leaves.

GINGER TEA

Stir 1/4 teaspoon ground ginger into a cup of hot water. Add sugar to taste (and lemon if desired).

Breads
&
Spreads

TEA SCONES

Scones are to tea what eggs are to breakfast. They are one of the first things that spring to mind when teatime is mentioned, and you'll almost certainly find them served at any establishment that offers afternoon tea. The Empress Hotel in Victoria, British Columbia, serves more than 80,000 teas a year. The menu always includes scones, along with goblets of fresh strawberries and cream chantilly, toasted honey crumpets, and an assortment of tea sandwiches. The setting at the Empress is elegant as well, with chintz wing chairs, loveseats, and lacquered tables all overlooking Victoria's inner harbor.

There are as many varieties of scones-
and as many ways to cook them—as there are
fish in the sea. This recipe comes from a Scottish
woman whose husband used to brag that she could have
a batch of scones in the oven between the time guests
entered their front gate and when they reached the front door.

2 cups unsifted all-purpose flour
1/2 cup sugar
2 tablespoons cream of tartar
1 teaspoon baking soda
3/4 teaspoon salt
1/2 cup shortening
1/2 cup raisins
2 eggs, slightly beaten
1/4 cup cold milk

Preheat oven to 400°F. Sift together dry ingredients. Cut in shortening with a pastry blender until mixture is the consistency of fine
bread crumbs. Add raisins, eggs, and milk; mix with a fork just to
blend. Divide dough into two parts. Turn half the dough out onto a
floured board; do not handle. Flatten with a rolling pin into a circle
about 1/2" thick. Cut into triangles and place on a greased and
floured baking sheet. Repeat for second half of dough. Bake 15 minutes, or until golden brown.

Notes: If you use a cookie cutter rather than cutting the scones into
triangles, do not twist the cutter; twisting causes the scones to be
lopsided. Scones are best eaten warm. They should be split along
their girth to expose the crumb face, and an area the size of one bite
spread with butter and jam.

BANANA-ORANGE MUFFIN CAKE

1 1/2 cups flour
1 cup uncooked rolled oats
1/3 cup packed brown sugar
1 tablespoon baking powder
1/2 teaspoon baking soda
1/4 teaspoon salt
2/3 cup mashed ripe banana
1/2 cup orange juice
1/3 cup melted butter
1 egg, lightly beaten
1/2 teaspoon grated orange zest
Glaze:
1/2 cup powdered sugar
1 tablespoon orange juice
1/2 teaspoon grated orange zest

Preheat oven to 400°F. Grease bottom of 9" round cake pan
or springform pan. Combine dry ingredients. Combine
banana, the 1/2 cup orange juice, butter, egg, and 1/2 teaspoon orange zest. Add liquid ingredients to dry ingredients; mix only enough to moisten dry ingredients. Pour
batter into pan; bake 30 to 35 minutes or until golden
brown. Cool 10 minutes before removing from pan.
Combine ingredients for glaze and drizzle over
warm cake.

ENGLISH MUFFINS

English muffins are almost too simple a tea food to mention, but too good not to. You can make English muffins at home, but it's a lot of fuss considering that Mr. Thomas makes such good ones. Be sure to use a fork to split the muffins. The nooks and crannies that result are a must for holding jams and jellies and giving the butter a place to puddle. Toast muffins under the broiler and top with luscious homemade or store-bought jams, or sprinkle the muffins with a mixture of brown sugar and cinnamon before broiling.

POPOVERS

1 cup flour
1 cup milk
3 tablespoons salad oil
1/2 teaspoon salt
3 eggs

Preheat oven to 400°F. Put all ingredients in a blender and blend well. Preheat greased muffin tins for 8 to 10 minutes before pouring the batter into them; fill about two-thirds to three-quarters full. Bake for 15 minutes, reduce heat to 350°F, and bake an additional 30 minutes. Do not open the oven door during the baking time, or the popovers won't pop. Makes 8 to 10 popovers.

MIM'S BANANA BREAD

This recipe was passed down by an "old college chum" of my mother-in-law and was popular with my son's friends, who appeared as if by magic whenever I baked it. They must have known that it was best hot out of the oven. From experience I know that it's impossible to fail with this recipe.

3 large or 4 small ripe bananas
1 cup sugar
1 egg
1 1/2 cups flour
1/4 cup melted butter
1 teaspoon baking soda
1 teaspoon salt

Preheat oven to 325°F. Butter and flour a 9" x 5" x 3" loaf pan. Mash bananas in a large bowl; add remaining ingredients and mix well. Pour batter into pan and bake 1 hour.

Note: Nuts or raisins may be added to the batter. You can also use this batter to make muffins, reducing the baking time.

ZUCCHINI BREAD

We used to have a garden, in which we planted a 79-cent packet of zucchini seeds each year. You know what happened—we had zucchini coming out of our ears. So as not to waste a penny of that 79 cents, I made a lot of this bread. It's delicious.

2 cups sugar
1 cup vegetable oil
3 eggs
1 tablespoon vanilla
2 1/2 cups unpeeled grated zucchini
cups flour
1 teaspoon baking soda
1/4 teaspoon baking powder
1 tablespoon cinnamon
Lots of raisins and/or nuts

Cream sugar, oil, and eggs. Add vanilla and zucchini. Blend dry ingredients and add to first mixture. Stir in raisins and/or nuts. Grease and flour two loaf pans, divide the mixture between the two pans, and bake at 350°F for 1 hour or until done.

Note: If you love cinnamon, increase the amount to 4 to 5 teaspoons. Coat the raisins with a little flour before adding to the batter, to keep them from sinking to the bottom. Use this batter for muffins, too.

APPLESAUCE CAKE

This cake was one of my mother's standbys.

1/2 cup shortening
1 cup sugar
2 eggs, beaten
1 cup thick applesauce
2 cups flour
1/2 teaspoon salt
1 teaspoon baking powder
1/2 teaspoon baking soda
1 teaspoon cinnamon
1/2 teaspoon ground cloves
1 cup raisins

Cream shortening and sugar, add eggs, and beat well. Add applesauce and all dry ingredients; beat until smooth. Fold in raisins. Bake in a greased 8" x 8" pan at 350°F for about 50 minutes. Insert a toothpick or a straw to test for doneness.

LEMON BUTTER

This spread makes any bread or roll taste even better than it
 already does.

1 cup granulated sugar
3 eggs
3 tablespoons butter
Juice and grated zest of one lemon

Beat all ingredients together and cook in the top of a double boiler
until thickened, stirring constantly. Place in a pretty crock, a cus-
tard cup, or a small mold. Chill.

LEMON-LIME CURD

If you're wild about the flavors of lemon and lime, this curd
makes a delicious spread or topping for just about anything.

2 large lemons
2 limes
3 eggs
1 cup sugar
1/2 cup (1 stick) unsalted butter, melted

Grate the zest from the lemons and limes; then squeeze and
reserve the juice. Place juice and zest in blender container; add
eggs and sugar. Cover and blend for a few seconds. With blender
running at medium speed, slowly add melted butter. Pour into a
heavy saucepan and cook over medium heat, stirring constantly,
until thickened.

FRUIT BUTTER

Combine 1/3 cup fruit preserves, 1/2 cup (1 stick) sweet butter (or salted butter will do just fine), 1 teaspoon lemon juice, and 1 teaspoon confectioners' sugar.

BUTTER CURLS

Butter curls, balls, or pats look especially nice for a tea. To make butter curls, start with a very cold stick of butter. Draw a butter curler across the stick, making a thin shaving of butter that will curl into a cylinder shape. Dip the curler into hot water immediately before making each curl.

To make butter balls, warm a melon baller and scoop cold butter into balls.

To make pats, cut neat squares from a stick of cold butter with a sharp knife dipped into cold water. To add decoration, dip a fork in hot water and draw it diagonally across each square.

As you make them, drop the butter curls, balls, or pats into a bowl of ice water. Refrigerate until ready to use. To serve, drain; arrange over ice.

JAMS AND JELLIES

If you make your own jams or jellies or have received fancy ones as gifts, be sure to serve them for tea. Any jam or jelly tastes better when served in a sparkling glass dish or a crystal goblet.

FRUIT PLATTER AND DIPS

Use your prettiest platter or any combination of serving dishes that suits your fancy to show off a luscious selection of fruit. Divided dishes are nice for pineapple spears, apple wedges, and strawberries. Combine the fruits or arrange them in a decorative manner. The more fruits, the better, but do offer at least four types. If you include apples and bananas, be sure to sprinkle them with lemon juice so they don't turn brown. Include some exotic fruits—kiwi, papaya, mango—if they're available in your market. Have a container of toothpicks nearby so that your guests can spear fruit chunks for dipping into one or both of the recipes on page 35.

PARMESAN CHEESE ROUNDS

36 rounds of party rye or pumpernickel bread
4 small onions, thinly sliced
1 cup mayonnaise
6 tablespoons Parmesan cheese

Under the broiler, toast the bread on one side. Turn; divide onions evenly over untoasted side of rounds. Mix mayonnaise and cheese; place a teaspoon of the mixture over the onion. Broil 3 to 5 minutes.

DIFFERENT CHEESE BALL

16 ounces cream cheese, softened
8 ounces crushed pineapple, drained
2 tablespoons finely chopped green onion (including tops)
1/4 to 1/2 cup finely chopped green or red peppers
1 teaspoon seasoned salt
2 cups chopped pecans

Mix cheese and pineapple. Stir in onion, peppers, salt, and 1/2 cup of the pecans. Roll into one large ball or two logs- or place in a scooped-out pineapple half. Roll or top with remaining pecans. Serve with bacon-flavored crackers.

Light

Servings

SPECIAL FRUIT SALAD

We all know how to make a fruit salad—mix together some melon balls, sliced bananas, grapes, berries, and whatever other fruits you enjoy. To make the salad special, however, toss it with Orange Cream Dressing (recipe follows), put it in a pretty bowl, and spread some whipped cream on top. Then arrange one or more of the specialty fruits—for example, papaya, star fruit, passion fruit, or mango—available at many markets over the whipped cream. Your guests will love it!

ORANGE CREAM DRESSING

1/2 cup mayonnaise
1/4 cup light corn syrup
1 tablespoon orange zest
1 tablespoon orange juice
1/4 teaspoon ground nutmeg
1/2 cup whipping cream, whipped

Mix mayonnaise and corn syrup until smooth. Add zest, juice, and nutmeg and stir well. Fold in whipped cream. Refrigerate.

YOGURT FRUIT DIP

1 cup plain yogurt
1 cup sour cream
2 tablespoons honey
3/4 teaspoon ground ginger
1/2 teaspoon lemon juice
Lemon zest (optional)

Blend all ingredients until smooth. Cover and refrigerate 1 hour or longer to chill and blend flavors. If you wish, sprinkle dip with lemon zest before serving.

PAM'S APPLE DIP

1/4 cup butter
3/4 cup brown sugar
1 cup sour cream
1/2 to 1 teaspoon vanilla

Melt butter. Add brown sugar and mix well. Blend in sour cream and vanilla. Chill before serving.

MARINATED MUSHROOMS

For simplicity, pour a bottle of purchased Italian salad dressing over whole mushrooms. Marinate several hours. If you prefer to make the marinade from scratch, try Patty's Marinated Mushrooms (recipe below).

PATTY'S MARINATED MUSHROOMS

1 pound mushrooms
1/2 cup olive oil
2 tablespoons tarragon vinegar
2 cloves garlic, crushed
1 teaspoon salt
1 teaspoon dry mustard
1/2 teaspoon sugar
1/4 teaspoon ground black pepper

Combine all ingredients. Marinate at least 1 hour.

PAPAYA AND SHRIMP BOATS

Cut papayas in half and remove the seeds. Scoop out and dice the papaya meat. Put some cottage cheese in each papaya "boat" and place chopped papaya on either side of it. Arrange several cooked shrimp over the edge and sprinkle with freshly ground black pepper. Serve on a plate of crushed ice.

CHUTNEY-CHICKEN TEA SANDWICHES

1 cup finely shredded cooked chicken breast
1/4 cup very finely diced celery (optional)
1/3 cup mayonnaise
2 tablespoons orange juice
3 tablespoons chutney
Dash curry powder
Salt (to taste)
16 thin slices good-quality white
or wholewheat bread
3 tablespoons unsalted butter (softened)

In a large bowl, combine chicken and celery. In a
small bowl, thoroughly combine mayonnaise,
orange juice, chutney (finely dice fruit pieces or
snip with kitchen shears), curry powder, and salt.
Add flavored mayonnaise to chicken mixture;
mix well.

Spread about 1/2 teaspoon butter on one side of
each of the bread slices. Divide sandwich filling
evenly among 8 of the slices. Top each with a
buttered bread slice. Trim crusts and cut sandwiches in half diagonally if desired. Makes 8
whole or 16 half sandwiches.

SMOKEY TURKEY-AVOCADO TEA SANDWICHES

Because they contain avocado, these sandwiches are best served soon after they are assembled.

16 thin slices whole-wheat bread
3 tablespoons unsalted butter (salted)
1 avocado, halved, seeded, peeled, and mashed
2 tablespoons lime juice
Dash Tabasco sauce
Salt and pepper (to taste)
8 thin slices deli smoked turkey breast
Watercress leaves

Spread about 1/2 teaspoon butter on one side of each of the bread slices; set aside. Thoroughly combine avocado, lime juice, and Tabasco; season to taste. Divide avocado mixture evenly among 8 of the buttered bread slices, spreading it just short of the edges. Top each with a slice of turkey, a few watercress leaves, and a buttered bread slice. Trim crusts and cut sandwiches in half diagonally if desired. Makes 8 whole or 16 half sandwiches.

BOSTON SANDWICHES

Here's something basic and earthy for a
special tea by the fire for your very best
friends-especially if your friends are from
New England.

1 cup cold baked beans, mashed
1 tablespoon chili sauce
1 teaspoon prepared mustard
Minced onion (as much as you like)

Combine all ingredients. Serve on Boston
brown bread or any good white bread.

SHELLFISH, BACON, AND EGG SANDWICHES

The ingredients serve four, but you can easily double or
triple the recipe for a larger crowd.

8 slices toast or toasted English muffin halves, buttered
3/4 cup uncooked minced bacon
1 onion, minced
1/2 cup chopped red, green, or yellow pepper
1 cup cleaned lobster, crab, or shrimp
8 eggs, slightly beaten
1/2 teaspoon salt
1/8 teaspoon freshly ground pepper

Arrange toast or muffins on a plate. Cook bacon until crisp.
Remove from pan and pour off some of the bacon grease. Add
onions and peppers and saute' until wilted or cooked to your taste.
Return bacon to pan; add shellfish to heat. Add eggs, salt, and pepper and cook, stirring, until eggs are scrambled to your liking. Serve
over toast or muffins.

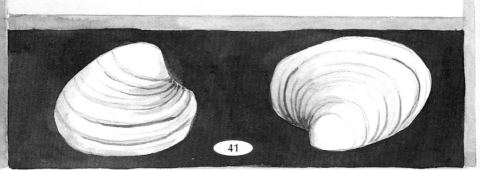

CURRY CASHEW SANDWICH SPREAD

This spread is very good on brown or whole wheat bread.

1 package (3 oz.) cream cheese, softened
1 tablespoon milk
1 teaspoon curry powder (less if you prefer)
1/4 cup chopped cashews

Into the cream cheese, blend first milk and then curry powder and nuts.

CUCUMBER AND SHRIMP SANDWICHES

1/3 cup shredded cucumber, drained well
1 cup chopped cooked shrimp
2 teaspoons minced green onion
1 1/2 teaspoons lemon juice
1/8 teaspoon dillweed
1/4 cup plain yogurt
Salt (to taste)
Sliced white bread, crusts removed
Butter

Thoroughly mix all ingredients except bread and butter. Spread bread slices with butter; then divide the sandwich filling among half the buttered slices. Top with another piece of buttered bread and cut into finger sandwiches.

Sweets

LIN WEBBER'S SHORTBREAD COOKIES

2 cups butter (do not substitute margarine)
1 cup sugar
1 teaspoon vanilla
5 cups flour

Cream butter and sugar. Add vanilla and mix well. Stir in flour by hand. Roll dough 1/2" thick; prick all over with fork. Cut into squares and place on a cookie sheet. Let sit 10 minutes before baking. Bake at 275°F for 45 minutes. Cool thoroughly and store in an airtight tin.

BENNE SEED WAFERS

Benne (better known as sesame seed)
was originally brought to America
from West Africa on the slave ships.
Among the descendants of those slaves
along the coast of South Carolina, legend has it that benne is a good luck
plant. This recipe is from Market Street
Munchies in Charleston.

3/4 cup softened butter
1 cup light brown sugar, packed
1 large egg
1/2 teaspoon vanilla
1 1/2 cups flour
1/2 teaspoon baking powder
1/2 cup benne (sesame seeds)

Cream butter and sugar; add egg and
vanilla and mix well. Stir in dry ingredients. Drop by half-teaspoon onto a
cookie sheet lined with waxed paper,
allowing room for wafers to spread.
Bake at 325°F for 10 minutes. Cool.
Store in a tightly sealed tin. Makes 6 to
8 dozen.

QUICK LEMON CRISPS

2 cups sifted flour
3/4 teaspoon baking soda
1/4 teaspoon salt
3/4 cup shortening
1 cup sugar
2 packages (each 3 3/4 oz.) lemon instant
pudding mix
3 eggs, slightly beaten

Sift together flour, baking soda, and salt; set
aside. Cream shortening and sugar. Add
pudding mix and cream until mixture is light
and fluffy. Add eggs; mix thoroughly. Add
dry ingredients and beat until well blended.
Drop from teaspoon onto greased baking
sheet about 2 1/2" apart. Bake at 375°F for 8
to 10 minutes. Makes about 6 dozen.

BUTTERSCOTCH BROWNIES

1/4 cup butter
1 cup brown sugar
1 egg
1/2 cup flour
1 teaspoon baking powder
1/2 teaspoon vanilla extract
1/4 cup chopped nuts (your choice)
1/4 cup coconut

Melt butter over low heat. Remove from heat, add brown sugar, and blend well. Stir in egg. Sift together flour and baking powder and stir into first mixture. Fold in remaining ingredients. Spread in a well-greased 8" x 8" x 2" pan. Bake at 350°F for 20 to 25 minutes. Brownies should be soft when removed from the oven so that the interior remains soft; they are not very thick. Cut into squares while warm.

GAM'S GRAHAM CRACKER CAKE

My grandmother was not a cook, but this recipe was passed down from her all the same. Mother always baked this cake for special occasions—garden club, bridge club, parties—and it was a hit each time she served it. Keep the cake away from small children who might be tempted, as my brother once was, to push the cherries down until they disappeared into the cake.

1/4 cup butter
1 cup sugar
2 eggs
2 teaspoons baking powder
2 cups crushed graham cracker crumbs
1 teaspoon vanilla extract
1 cup milk
1 cup chopped walnuts
1 pint whipping cream
Maraschino cherries

Preheat oven to 350°F. Cream butter and sugar until smooth. Add eggs and beat well. Mix baking powder with crumbs; add to creamed mixture. Add vanilla, milk, and nuts; mix well. Grease and flour two 8" round cake pans, and divide the batter between them. Bake 20 minutes or until a toothpick inserted in the cake comes out clean. Cool before removing from pans. Beat whipping cream and frost cake with it. Arrange cherries over the top.

Note: This cake can be a bit difficult to remove from the pans. If it breaks, the whipped cream will hide everything. Consider investing in cake pans that have a turn blade built into them. They're difficult to find but are worth their weight in gold. The more whipped cream you use, the better, because it soaks into the cake.

ICEBOX CAKE

This cake was a family favorite when I was young. When I fix it for friends, they suddenly remember it from their childhood, too.

To make this icebox cake, you need chocolate cookie wafers, which can be difficult to find in some stores. They used to be square and sold in the cookie section. Now they're round, and you'll usually find them on the shelves in the ice cream section. You'll need at least two boxes and a pint of heavy whipping cream. You must prepare this cake at least a day before serving.

Whip the cream. Spread a little on one side of a wafer. Repeat, stacking the wafers on their sides on a sheet of waxed paper to form a roll. If you like, reserve enough of the whipped cream to cover the edges of the wafers. Save one or two wafers, break into fine crumbs, and sprinkle the crumbs over the top of the cake. This cake must rest in the refrigerator at least overnight for the wafers to soften as they absorb moisture from the whipped cream. Cut the cake on the diagonal.

HEAVENLY FUDGE

2 cups sugar
2 tablespoons light corn syrup
3/4 cup milk
2 squares unsweetened chocolate
2 tablespoons butter
1 teaspoon vanilla

In a heavy saucepan, heat sugar, syrup, milk, and chocolate, stirring until sugar is dissolved. Continue cooking, without stirring, until a small amount of the mixture forms a soft ball when dropped into very cold water. Remove from heat and stir in butter. Let cool. (It's cool when you can hold your hand on the bottom of the pan.) Add vanilla, beat well, and pour fudge into a greased pan. When cool, cut into squares.

SHORTCAKE

Everyone has a shortcake recipe, but this is the best one I've found.

2 cups flour
1 teaspoon baking powder
1 teaspoon salt
2 tablespoons sugar
6 tablespoons butter or vegetable shortening
I egg
3/4 cup miLk

Mix the above ingredients and pour into an 8" by 8" pan. Bake for 30 minutes at 450°F. Use hot or cold, topped with whipped cream and strawberries. I find alot of people prefer this with milk or cream, because the shortbread soaks it up and becomes even better.

STRAWBERRY TORTE

This is a recipe from Pam, and when berries are in season, you can always count on her to present this on any occasion

20 Ritz crackers, crushed
3/4 cup granulated sugar
1 cup finely chopped pecans
1/2 teaspoon vanilla
3 egg whites
1/4 cup granulated sugar

Combine cracker crumbs, the 3/4 cup sugar, pecans, and vanilla. Beat the egg whites with the 1/4 cup sugar until stiff; fold into the cracker mixture. Divide mixture; spread in two 8" rounds on buttered cookie sheets. Bake 25 minutes at 350°F. Cool completely and remove from sheets. Place sliced strawberries (Pam suggests that you add sugar to the strawberries) on these meringue crusts and cover with whipped cream.

RASPBERRY SAUCE

In a blender or food processor, puree one 10-ounce
package of frozen raspberries (thawed) and 1/2 cup
sugar (omit the sugar if the berries are already sweet-
ened). Combine a little of this mixture with 1 tablespoon cornstarch in a small saucepan. Add remaining
puree and cook, stirring constantly, until thickened.
Cool. Pour over Raspberry Squares.

Note: This sauce is also great over ice cream or
brownies or both.

RASPBERRY SQUARES

Every year we get together with four other couples a few weeks before Christmas for a cookie bake. Even the men have to make their own batch of cookies. These squares are just one of the creations we've turned out.

1/2 cup butter
3/4 cup sugar (divided)
2 eggs, separated
1 1/2 cups flour
1/2 teaspoon salt
Raspberry jam
1 teaspoon vanilla extract
1/2 cup chopped nuts (your choice)

Cream butter and 1/4 cup of the sugar. Add egg yolks, beating well. Stir in flour and salt. Spread mixture in a greased 8" x 8" x 2" pan. Carefully spread jam over batter. Beat egg whites until stiff, adding remaining 1/2 cup sugar and the vanilla as they thicken. Spread egg white mixture over jam. Sprinkle with the nuts. Bake at 350°F for 30 minutes. Cool and cut into squares.
Top with Raspberry Sauce (recipe on page 52).

Index

Index

Between Friends®
COOKBOOK SERIES

Titles Currently Available:

Afternoon Teas
The ultimate gift book! Browse through these beautiful pages while reading about the history of teas and the tea ceremony - then plan your own special event.
Recipes from simple to elegant, yet practical for today's cook. A variety of suggested menus are presented with all recipes included inside. This finely-appointed book is sure to become a favorite.

Afternoon Teas
ISBN #1-56523-040-X
Perfectbound, 64 pages, watercolors throughout.
$7.95

The Fireside Cookbook
Look inside this book for a wonderful collection of ideas and recipes for hosting creative dinners. From romantic dining to family get-togethers, this is a delicious and fun cookbook. Includes sample menus and hints for such themed dinners as New Years Eve, Colonial Williamsburg Style, Snowstorm Dinner and more.
Exquisite watercolors shine from every page, making this book a treasure to keep or give.

Fireside Dining
ISBN #1-56523-041-8
Perfectbound, 64 pages, 5.5 x 8.5, watercolors throughout.
$7.95

Available from all bookstores
and fine gift shops.

If you cannot find these titles at your favorite store you may order by mail.
Please send $7.95 + $1.00 postage to:

Fox Chapel Book Orders
Box 7948
Lancaster, PA 17604-7948